Meet My
AFRICA

BY AYO WILSON
ILLUSTRATED BY DOHA KOMA

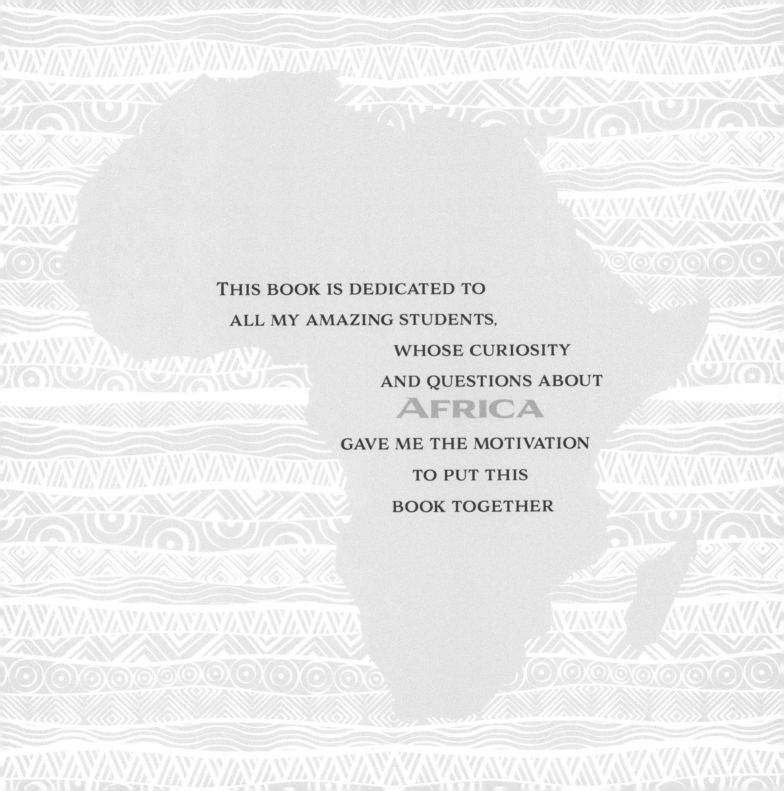

THIS BOOK IS DEDICATED TO
ALL MY AMAZING STUDENTS,
WHOSE CURIOSITY
AND QUESTIONS ABOUT
AFRICA
GAVE ME THE MOTIVATION
TO PUT THIS
BOOK TOGETHER

Come and meet my **AFRICA**, a world of many faces,
where everybody welcomes you with smiles and warm embraces.
A continent of cultures, blended languages, great minds,
home to iconic animals—we have so many kinds!

See the Sahara Desert, Atlas Mountains, River Nile—
come, let's meet my AFRICA, you'll leave here with a smile.

AFRICA IS A CONTINENT THAT'S FULL OF MANY NATIONS,
RICH WITH LANDMARKS, HABITATS, AND SUCH DIVERSE LOCATIONS.

Did you know AFRICA
is the second-largest
continent in the world
and there are over 50 different
countries in it?

The Serengeti in **Tanzania** is the world's largest savannah. Each year it plays host to the largest overland migration on Earth of over 1.5 million blue wildebeest and hundreds of thousands of zebra and gazelle.

The Sahara is also called **"the Great Desert"** for being the largest hot desert in the world. It is home to many animals, including fennec foxes, deathstalker scorpions, and red-necked ostriches.

The **Congo** rainforest is the second largest rainforest in the world after the Amazon. It spans across six African countries—**Democratic Republic of the Congo, Cameroon, Central African Republic, Republic of the Congo, Equatorial Guinea**, and **Gabon**.

Some of Africa's biggest cities include Kinshasa in the **Democratic Republic of the Congo,** Cairo in **Egypt,** Lagos in **Nigeria,** Abidjan in **Côte d'Ivoire,** Johannesburg in **South Africa,** Casablanca in **Morocco,** and Luanda in **Angola.** Big cities are always bustling and full of many people doing different jobs to help their communities.

Villages in **AFRICA** are calm, and farming is the main occupation and source of income for the people, just like Davedi village in **Togo**, well-known for its big pineapple fields and palm trees.

Did you know that one of the world's oldest learning institutions, Sankore University, also called Sankore Madrasah, was created in Timbuktu, **Mali?**

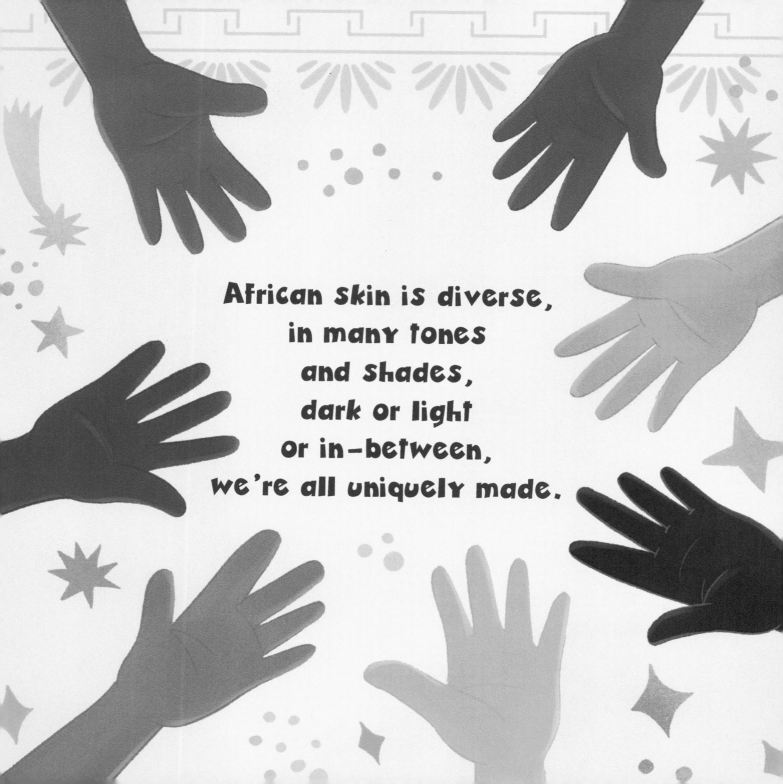

African skin is diverse,
in many tones
and shades,
dark or light
or in-between,
we're all uniquely made.

AND WE STYLE OUR HAIR IN MANY DIFFERENT WAYS,
CURLY, FLUFFY, LONG OR SHORT, STRAIGHT OR EVEN BRAIDS.

THOUSANDS OF AFRICAN LANGUAGES AND SO MANY WORDS TO SAY—
THEY'RE ALL UNIQUE AND SPOKEN IN THEIR OWN DISTINCTIVE WAY.

Did you know that there are
over two thousand languages
spoken in AFRICA, and
most Africans speak more
than one language?

From Yoruba to Wolof, Tamasheq to Chewa, Amharic to Swati, Fon to Baoulé, the list of languages spoken in AFRICA goes on and on!

AFRICA is a continent of many cultures, beliefs, and religions. While most Christians across Africa love to celebrate Christmas and Easter, Muslims celebrate Eid-al-Fitr and Eid al-Adha. There are also traditional religious celebrations such as Bwiti ceremony in Gabon and festival of masks in Burkina Faso.

Africans have a rich tradition of oral storytelling. The stories are meant to teach morals, entertain, and transfer customs and traditions from one generation to another. In **Mauritania**, **Senegal**, and **Mali**, storytellers —also known as griots—use music to tell their stories.

The Iri-Ji, or **"New Yam Festival,"** is an annual traditional thanksgiving festival among the Igbo people in Nigeria and one of the most celebrated cultural events in Africa. It's a special time for celebrating the beginning and end of the farming season, personal achievements, and good health with a lot of food, dancing, singing, and prayers.

WITHOUT A TASTY FEAST, NO CELEBRATION IS COMPLETE—
ALWAYS COLORFUL AND DELICIOUS WITH A LITTLE BIT OF HEAT!

Most of the food that Africans eat is grown in **AFRICA**,
and every country and region has its own special dishes
with unique flavors and methods of making them.
Most dishes include cornmeal, rice, porridge,

vegetables, meat, and spices.

AFRICA IS WHERE MOST OF THE WORLD'S COCOA IS GROWN AND SOLD, AS WELL AS SPARKLING DIAMONDS—AND LET'S NOT FORGET GOLD!

AFRICA is the highest producer of cocoa beans in the world, so the cocoa in the chocolate you eat likely comes from here.

Did you know that many diamonds in the world come from AFRICA?

These diamonds are found in countries such as **Botswana, Democratic Republic of the Congo, Angola, South Africa, Zimbabwe, Namibia, Sierra Leone,** and **Guinea.**

AFRICAN ANIMALS VARY IN THEIR COLORS, SHAPES, AND SIZES.
THEY'RE EASIEST TO SPOT AT NIGHT OR AS THE WARM SUN RISES.

CHEETAHS are the world's fastest land mammal, and they live in **AFRICA**. They run faster than even a sports car! Cheetahs have a long tail that helps them maintain balance and make quick turns. A cheetah can run only about 30 seconds at a time before it needs to stop and rest.

GIRAFFES

are the tallest animal in the world and can grow up to 19 feet high. They can be found in African savannahs, grasslands, and open woodlands.

LIONS

are known as **"King of the Beasts"** because they are so strong and fierce. Nearly all wild lions live in Africa. Females do most of the hunting. They are the only cats that live with their family in groups called "prides."

ELEPHANTS

are highly intelligent animals and can live up to 70 years! African elephants are the largest land animal on Earth. Their large ears are **shaped like the continent of Africa.**

Lions, leopards, buffalo, rhinos, and elephants are known as "The Big Five" in AFRICA. Sadly, these Big Five are endangered. Lions and leopards are considered some of the most difficult and dangerous African animals to hunt, so some people kill them for sport.

Rhinoceroses and elephants especially are sadly hunted by some people for their horns and tusks, which they use to make ornaments and medicine.

Did you know the Great Pyramid in Cairo, **Egypt**, is the only structure out of the Seven Wonders of the Ancient World that still exist? It was built as a tomb for king Khufu over 4,500 years ago and took more than 20 years to build.

Have you heard of Mount Kilimanjaro in **Tanzania**? It is the highest mountain in AFRICA, and also the highest free-standing mountain in the world.

Victoria Falls, located between **Zambia** and **Zimbabwe**, is known as one of the widest waterfalls in the world. It is even wider than Niagara Falls in North America.

The Republic of Madagascar is a beautiful island country in AFRICA and is also the second-largest island country in the world. Most of the plants and animals that are found in Madagascar exist nowhere else on Earth.

The River Nile flows through eleven different African countries— **Ethiopia, Sudan, South Sudan, Democratic Republic of the Congo, Tanzania, Rwanda, Uganda, Burundi, Eritrea, Kenya,** and **Egypt**—and is about 6,650 kilometers long!

AFRICAN WEAVING, PAINTING, AND FILMS ARE NOT OUR ONLY ART—
LISTEN TO AFRICAN MUSIC AND ITS SOUND WILL MELT YOUR HEART!

Music: Music and dance are an integral part of African culture. African music is catchy, melodious, and energetic. Incredible international music festivals are held in various countries across Africa, welcoming people from all over the world. **Afrobeats, Gospel, Taarab, Mbalax, Amapiano, Makossa, Coupé-Décalé, Raï, Funaná,** and **Highlife** are some of the popular types of music in AFRICA. Our musical instruments include the djembe drum, korra, balafon, shekere, bendir, udu, and gangan.

Film: **Did you know that the Nigerian film industry, known as "Nollywood," is one of the largest film industries in the world?**

Fashion: African fashion is known for its beautiful, vibrant colors and bold prints which are rooted in cultural heritage. A few examples of African fabrics include ankara, kente, and bògòlanfini.

Ankara, also known as Dutch wax, is very popular in **AFRICA** because of its colorful prints and versatility. Many different clothing and fashion accessories are made with ankara fabric.

Kente is a traditional cloth from **Ghana** worn primarily for celebrations. Every color used in the cloth carries its own meaning, so people like to design their own patterns. Kente was said to have started in a town called Bonwire, where two young men learned how to weave the cloth simply by observing a spider spinning its web.

Bògòlanfini, or "mud cloth," originated from **Mali** and is woven by men while women take care of the dyeing process by mixing mud and different vegetation together to create a variety of colors.

Nelson Mandela is one of the greatest peacemakers in history. He led the fight against Apartheid in **South Africa** so that everyone would be treated fairly and equally, regardless of the color of their skin. As well as winning the 1993 Nobel Peace Prize, he also became South Africa's first democratically elected black head of state between 1994 and 1999.

Kofi Annan from **Ghana** was the Secretary-General of the United Nations between 1997 and 2006, helping people and countries to work together peacefully. He won the 2001 Nobel Peace Prize for working hard for a better organized and more peaceful world. Kofi Annan spoke many languages fluently, including Akan, English, French, and other African languages.

Wangari Muta Maathai encouraged people to plant millions of trees in **Kenya** and help slow down deforestation. She believed anyone—man or woman—can save the world. In 2004, she became the first African woman to win the Nobel Peace Prize.

Chinua Achebe from Nigeria was one of the world's leading writers. His novel **Things Fall Apart** has been translated into more than 50 different languages. He received numerous awards and honors from around the world and is known as the "Father of African Literature."

Now you've met my AFRICA,
our doors are always open,
the people here are so diverse with bonds
that can't be broken.

Africa, our home, the place we love and hold so dear,
the land that is so beautiful it makes
our big hearts cheer.

Come again, my friends,
to where the sun
is warm and bright,
we welcome you
to AFRICA
with joy and
great delight.

FLAGS OF AFRICA

Algeria

Angola

Benin

Botswana

Chad

Comoros

Democratic Republic of the Congo

Republic of the Congo

Ethiopia

Gabon

Gambia

Ghana

Libya

Madagascar

Malawi

Mali

Niger

Nigeria

Rwanda

São Tomé and Príncipe

South Sudan

Sudan

Swaziland

Tanzania

Burkina Faso	Burundi	Cameroon	Cape Verde	Central African Republic
Côte d'Ivoire	Djibouti	Egypt	Equatorial Guinea	Eritrea
Guinea	Guinea-Bissau	Kenya	Lesotho	Liberia
Mauritania	Mauritius	Morocco	Mozambique	Namibia
Senegal	Seychelles	Sierra Leone	Somalia	South Africa
Togo	Tunisia	Uganda	Zambia	Zimbabwe

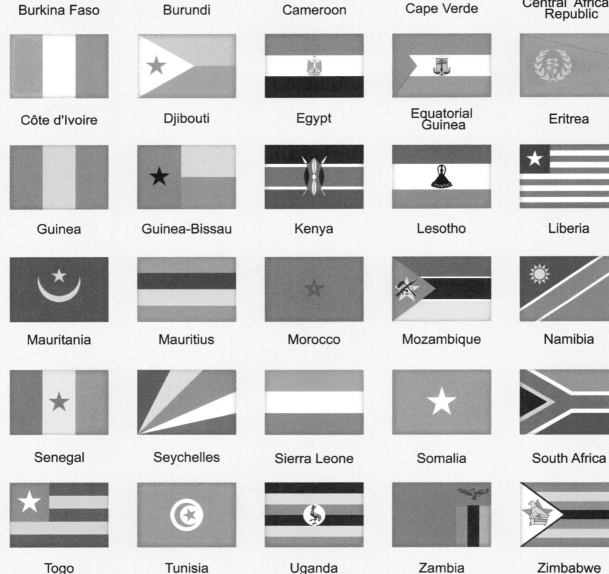

ABOUT THE AUTHOR

AYO WILSON is a proud and passionate African. She is a Montessori teacher and an Early Childhood Educator in Welland, Ontario, where she lives with her husband and children. Originally from **Nigeria**, she has explored and lived in a few other African countries, such as Mali, where she started her family and teaching career in 2005. Ayo speaks four languages and enjoys sharing her knowledge about this vast and unique continent with young learners.

One Printers Way
Altona, MB R0G 0B0
Canada

www.friesenpress.com

ISBN
978-1-03-918068-0 (Hardcover)
978-1-03-918067-3 (Paperback)
978-1-03-918069-7 (eBook)

1. JUVENILE NONFICTION, PEOPLE & PLACES, AFRICA

Distributed to the trade by The Ingram Book Company

Printed in the USA
CPSIA information can be obtained
at www.ICGtesting.com
LVHW071333120424
777208LV00018B/370

9 781039 180673